M000028904

OTHER BOOKS IN THIS SERIES:
"I paint as a bird sings" – Art Quotations
"Dance is the air we breathe" – Dance Quotations
"Music is the voice of all sorrow, all joy" – Music Quotations

Front cover quotation: Anonymous Native American.

Published simultaneously in 1998 by Exley Publications Ltd
in Great Britain, and Exley Publications LLC in the USA.

12 11 10 9 8 7 6 5 4 3 2 1

Editor: Claire Lipscomb. Series Editor: Helen Exley.
Copyright © Helen Exley 1998
The moral right of the author has been asserted.

ISBN 1-86187-530-4

Exley Publications Ltd, 16 Chalk Hill, Watford, Herts WD19 4BG, UK.
Exley Publications LLC, 185 Main Street, Spencer MA 01562, USA.
www.helenexleygiftbooks.com

Acknowledgements: The publishers are grateful for permission to reproduce copyright material. Whilst
every reasonable effort has been made to trace copyright holders, the publishers would be pleased to
hear from any not here acknowledged. STEPHEN BROOK: From the introduction to Opera: A
Penguin Anthology, edited by Stephen Brook. © Stephen Brook 1995. PAUL CLAUDEL: From
Modern Drama and Music, Yale Review, 1930. AMELITA GALLI-CURCI: From The Last Prima
Donnas by Lanfranco Rasponi, published by Gollancz. © 1984. LESLEY GARRETT: Extracts from
interviews in Mail on Sunday, Night and Day magazine February 1998; Executive Woman, July/August
1997 and Express on Sunday, Boulevard magazine, June 1997. WERNER HERZOG: From Plácido
Domingo's Tales from the Opera, published by BBC Books, London. © 1994 Daniel Snowman.
WAYNE KOESTENBAUM: From The Queen's Throat: Opera and Homosexuality and the Mystery of
of Desire, published by Gay Men's Press. © 1993. FIONA MADDOCKS: From "A voice only the
angels can explain" from Independent, June 1991. SHERRILL MILNES: From Bravo by Helena
Matheopoulos, published by Weidenfeld and Nicholson 1986. LUCIANO PAVAROTTI: From
Pavarotti: My World by Luciano Pavarotti and William Wright, published by Chatto and Windus. ©
1995 Worldwide Concert Corporation and William Wright. JOANNA PITMAN: From The Times
Magazine, October 1995. LIBBY PURVES: From "Personally Speaking" in Woman and Home, June
1998. DANIEL SNOWMAN: From Plácido Domingo's Tales from the Opera, by Daniel Snowman,
published by BBC Books, London. © 1994 Daniel Snowman. PAM BROWN, CHARLOTTE GRAY:
published with permission © Helen Exley 1998. Picture Credits: Exley Publications is very grateful
to the following individuals and organizations for permission to reproduce their pictures: AISA, Archiv
Für Kunst (AKG), Art Resource (AR), Bridgeman Art Library (BAL), Fine Art Photographic Library
(FAP), Giraudon (GIR), Image Select International (IS), Scala (SC), Superstock (SS). Cover: Gustav
Klimt, The Auditorium of the Old Castle Theatre, BAL; Title-page: William Powell Frith, At the Opera,
BAL; p6: SC; pp8/9: SC/AR; p10: BAL; p12: BAL; pp14/15: GIR/AR; p16: BAL; p19: FAP; pp20/21:
BAL; p22: BAL; pp24/25: GIR/BAL; p27: GIR/AR; p29: SS; p31: IS; p32: AKG; p35: BAL; p36: AKG;
p39: BAL; pp40/41: AISA; p42: BAL; p44: BAL; p47: AKG; pp48/49: SS; p50: BAL; pp52/53: SS; p54:
SS; pp56/57: SC/AR; p58: AR; p60: AKG.

"*Sing your song looking up at the sky*"

OPERA QUOTATIONS

A HELEN EXLEY GIFTBOOK

OVERLEAF: "INTERIOR OF THE SCALA THEATRE WITH THE STAGE CURTAIN OF MONTICELLI"

"**O**pera is a dramatic and lyric work of art combining all charms of the fine arts in a passionate action in order to arouse sympathy and illusion by means of pleasant sense perceptions. The composite parts of the opera are the poem, music, and decoration. Poetry speaks to the mind, music to the ear, painting to the eyes; and all must become one to move the heart."
JEAN-JACQUES ROUSSEAU (1712-1778)

"I was attracted to opera in the first place, because of the music and the spectacle. Where else does the curtain rise to reveal designs by Hockney or gowns by Armani? Then you have the acting, dancing and singing. At its best, I feel that opera is the greatest, all round, artistic experience you can have...."
LESLEY GARRETT

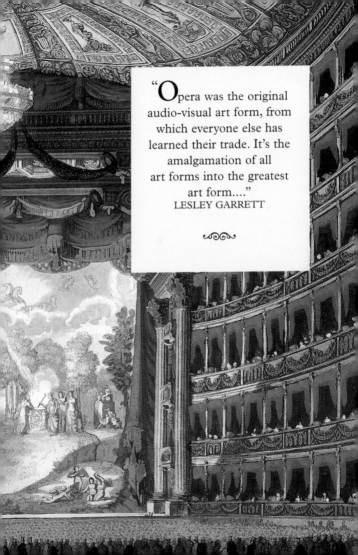

"Opera was the original audio-visual art form, from which everyone else has learned their trade. It's the amalgamation of all art forms into the greatest art form...."
LESLEY GARRETT

"**I** was born to sing."
JOSÉ CARRERAS, b.1946

❧❧❧

"If I cannot sing, I have the impression that
I no longer exist. I mean it.
I mean that I am not physically there."
MONTSERRAT CABALLÉ

❧❧❧

"Singing is my passion. I feel such a wonderful,
uplifting kind of joy when I sing, it's as if I am flying. I
can swoop and dive and leap about in song. I can
sweep through the whole range of emotions in song. I
can live in my song and that is why I love it."
CECILIA BARTOLI

❧❧❧

ABOVE: Constantin Dmitrievitch Flavitsky, "Princess Tarakanov"

PREVIOUS PAGE: Alois Hans Schram, "Gypsy Girl with a Tambourine"

"**O**pera is about life and everything that entails – love, hate and passion."
LESLEY GARRETT

"Opera encapsulates human emotions in their most distilled, elemental form, like the axioms of mathematics, reducible no further. That's why operatic emotions are so stylized – and so powerful. Opera involves danger, chaos, havoc, taking people to their limits and maybe beyond."
WERNER HERZOG,
from *Plácido Domingo's Tales from the Opera*, by Daniel Snowman

"The opera must draw tears, terrify people, make them die through singing."
VINCENZO BELLINI (1801-1835)

Edouard Joseph Dantan, "A Premiere at the Comedie Francaise in 1855"

C C C C C

"**O**pera lovers are fanatical
because when a performance
is great, it's the
most exhilarating experience
in the world
outside the bedroom."
STEPHEN BROOK

လာရှိသာ

"Opera comes to me before
anything else."
WOLFGANG AMADEUS MOZART
(1756-1791)

လာရှိသာ

"Not an audience but a habit."
GIAN CARLO MENOTTI,
on patrons of the Metropolitan Opera,
quoted in *Time*, May 1, 1950

လာရှိသာ

C C C C C

©1998 Fermin Rocker, "The Orchestra Pit–The Overture"

"**S**ome say that the best part of an opera is the anticipation. House lights. Orchestra. Curtain up onto a world of wonder."
PAM BROWN, b.1928

❦

"The maestro takes his seat at the piano. The house is packed with people who have poured in from twenty miles around. ...The overture begins, and you could hear a pin drop."
STENDHAL (1783-1842)

❦

"The musicians filed in one after the other, and there began a prolonged din of rumbling double-basses, creaking violins, barking cornets, and chirruping flutes and flageolets. From the stage came the sound of three knocks to signal the performance was about to begin. The drums began to roll...."
GUSTAVE FLAUBERT (1821-1880), from *Madame Bovary*

"Opera is a bizarre mixture of poetry and music where the writer and the composer, equally embarrassed by each other, go to a lot of trouble to create an execrable work."
SIEUR DE SAINT-EVREMOND

⌘

"I have sat through an Italian opera, till, for sheer pain, and inexplicable anguish, I have rushed out into the noisiest places of the crowded streets, to solace myself with sounds which I was not obliged to follow, and get rid of the distracting torment of endless, fruitless, barren attention!"
CHARLES LAMB (1775-1834)

⌘

"Going to the opera, like getting drunk, is a sin that carries its own punishment."
HANNAH MORE

Franz Skarbina, "An Evening Stroll"

Gustav Klimt, "The Auditorium of the Old Castle Theatre"

"Any great work of art...
revives and readapts time and
space, and the measure of its
success is the extent to which
it makes you an inhabitant of
that world – the extent to
which it invites you in and lets
you breathe its strange,
special air."
LEONARD BERNSTEIN

୭ଡ଼ଡ଼ଡ଼

"Opera is a divine illusion
whereby a theatre of strangers
is bound together in a common
experience bewitched into the
belief that all before them is
reality writ large.
Sharing in music the grief and joy
of people who live out of time
yet speak directly to our own."
PAM BROWN, b.1928

Henri de Toulouse-Lautrec, "Scene from 'The Messaline' at Bordeaux Opera"

Overleaf: Alexandre Cabanel, "Francesca da Rimini and Paolo Malatesta"

"All great singers feel themselves to be part of a great mystery, in which they are constantly aware of the arbitrariness of a cosmos which has endowed them with this gift...."
MARTIN KETTLE,
from the *Guardian,* July 4, 1992

☙❧

"The mystique of an internationally acclaimed singer is unlike that of any other virtuoso musician. We can see skill at work in a violinist or pianist and attribute our own inability to fat fingers or bad co-ordination. With a singer, we see nothing but an open mouth. In theory, we should all be able to sing. That we cannot makes us yet more in awe."
FIONA MADDOCKS,
from the *Independent,* June 15, 1991

☙❧

"... music can communicate the feeling of romantic love with a sudden power and glory not possible even to Shakespeare in *Romeo*. Some of Beaumarchais's people say they love; Mozart's people give off love in sound...."
ERIC BENTLEY

"… there can be something almost ritualistic about a powerful performance of *Norma, Aida, Parsifal* or *Turandot*, a formalized re-enactment of a great mythic story created by a revered figure from the past, in which our visual and aural imagination is stimulated by powerful emotions of a transcendent nature. The emotional catharsis involved is akin to that experienced by the devout in church."

DANIEL SNOWMAN, from *Plácido Domingo's Tales from the Opera*

"The great thing… about opera, is that it deals with timeless passions. In some ways, this is an antidote to our technology-obsessed society. It's wonderful to tap into those huge emotions. I often think that if more people went to the opera, there would be less need for psychoanalysts!"

LESLEY GARRETT

"**W**hen you sing you give everything; you are squeezed out like a lemon. It is wonderful."
MONTSERRAT CABALLÉ

✵✵✵

"For me, what makes singing exciting is the idea that you are communicating not just the composer's intentions, not the emotions of the character you are portraying, but also part of your own nature that cannot come out in other ways."
LUCIANO PAVAROTTI, b.1935, from *Pavarotti: My World*

✵✵✵

" ... for singers; their musical instrument... is an integral part of their own bodies. ... a singer reveals his or her very essence – all the physical, intellectual, and musical impulses in the artistic armoury – the moment work begins."
DANIEL SNOWMAN, from *Plácido Domingo's Tales from the Opera*

ABOVE: ©1998 BERNARD DUNSTAN, "KATHLEEN FERRIER AT A CONCERT"

PREVIOUS PAGE: GIOVANNI PAOLO PANNINI, "MUSICAL FETE GIVEN BY CARDINAL DE LA ROCHEFOUCAULD AT THEATRE ARGENTINA, ROME ON JULY 15, 1747"

"Opera appreciation becomes obsessive because no two performances are ever the same. This is true of the theatre as well, but there are more variables in the opera house: the temper of the conductor, the lungs of the tenor, the wakefulness of the lighting director, the sobriety of the orchestra."
STEPHEN BROOK

"Opera can delight the heart and mind
in a hall, in a small theatre,
in a vast opera house,
in the grounds of a mansion,
in a Roman amphitheatre.
Each performance is created by audience and
performers and venue –
and so each is utterly unique."
PAM BROWN, b.1928

ABOVE: AROLDO BONZAGNI, "BALL AT SCALA"

PREVIOUS PAGE: "THE THEATRE BOX", AFTER THE PAINTING BY PIERRE AUGUSTE RENOIR

"Opera: An exotic and irrational entertainment."
DR. SAMUEL JOHNSON (1709-1784)

꩜

"[Opera] is a concert in fancy dress, the intervals and transitions of which are more or less filled up by some vague noise. Only, in a concert, the singers can stand motionless if they choose, while in an opera they feel bound to indulge in conventional, ridiculous gestures...."
PAUL CLAUDEL, from *Modern Drama and Music*

꩜

"As for operas, they are essentially too absurd and extravagant to mention; I look upon them as a magic scene, contrived to please the eyes and the ears, at the expense of the understanding.... Whenever I go to an opera, I leave my sense and reason at the door with my half guinea...."
LORD CHESTERFIELD (1694-1773)

"There are those who mock the artificiality of opera. It's easy to do, and there is no rational defence. If you find the whole thing risible, laugh away – and stay away. Opera lovers know, indeed, that the formal constraints of opera, its supposedly absurd conventions, can heighten rather than diminish its impact. Of course people don't sing their opinions or conversations 'in real life'. That is the whole point of opera. It articulates in glorious music what we 'in real life' can only stutter in semi-articulate prose. A declaration of love, beneath a visiting moon or even on a theatrical stage, is confined by the limited number of words at the disposal of those making it. But the operatic love scene has no such constraints: it confers immortality on an everyday occurrence."
STEPHEN BROOK

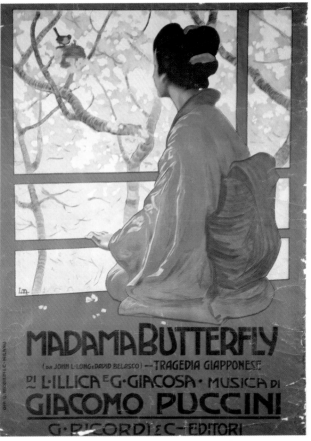

"Frontispiece to the Music Score for 'Madame Butterfly' by Giacomo Puccini"

"TITLE PAGE OF 'TURANDOT' MUSIC SCORE"

"... the voice... must be subordinate, it must only be the foundation, the soil from which flowers true art."
LOTTE LEHMANN (1888-1976)

❧◉◎◎

"... it isn't enough that you have a beautiful voice; you must take this voice and break it up into a thousand pieces, so she will serve you."
MARIA CALLAS (1923-1977)

❧◉◎◎

"... although you can tell whether the voice will be somewhere within the area of normal, you can't be sure of *exactly* how the sound will come out, until after it happens. It is an entity within ourselves, dependent yet also independent, and never wholly controllable. In fact it feels almost like a third person...."
SHERRILL MILNES

❧◉◎◎

"... when you conduct opera, you've got two sets of forces to control at once, the singers 'upstairs' and the players 'downstairs'. 'It's like being a Roman gladiator,' he [Domingo] laughed.... 'You've got one leg in one chariot pulled by a hundred horses in one direction, and the other in another chariot pulled by another hundred horses in a different direction!' The sheer effort involved in keeping all those horses under control is one of the hardest jobs an operatic conductor is called upon to do. If he fails, he will be torn apart by the various powerful forces nominally at his command. If he succeeds, he will have the chance to preside over one of those glorious, multifaceted musical ensembles that constitute opera at its grandest."

DANIEL SNOWMAN,
from *Plácido Domingo's Tales from the Opera*

EDGAR DEGAS, " 'ROBERTO IL DIABOLO': SET DESIGN"

OVERLEAF: FERDINAND KRUIS, "EVENING AT THE NEW MARKET"

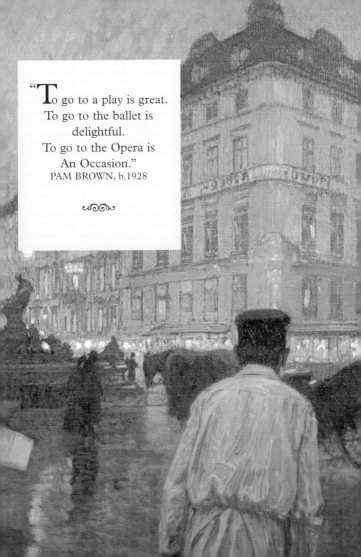

"To go to a play is great.
To go to the ballet is
delightful.
To go to the Opera is
An Occasion."
PAM BROWN, b.1928

GEORGES LABADIE PILOTELL, "GIUSEPPE VERDI (1813-1901), CARICATURE"

"Those people on the stage are making such a noise I
can't hear a word you're saying."
HENRY TAYLOR PARKER,
American music critic,
to some talkative members of an audience

∞∞∞

"One evening a lady in the audience at New York's
Metropolitan Opera House, leant over the front of the
stalls and asked the conductor, 'I wonder whether you
would be able to play the third act before the second
tonight? My friend and I have to catch a train, you see,
and we do so want to know how it all ends.'"
from *Off-Beat*,
Dudley Moore's Book of Musical Anecdotes

∞∞∞

©1998 Roma Ribera, "Lady with a Mask"

"It is the destiny of the coloratura to be like an acrobat on a steel wire. The public waits anxiously to see if you are going to crack on a certain note or be unable to finish a certain difficult *filatura,* just like the public in a circus follows attentively to see if the poor wretch is going to miss a jump and fall below."
AMELITA GALLI-CURCI (1882-1963)

❦

"The audience is excited by the danger that hysterical or extreme parts pose to the voice: opera requires the preservation of a singing instrument, and yet opera also explodes the boundaried, obedient self, moving listeners and performers away from respectability and towards rage, even if the throat is silenced by the travail of speaking out."
WAYNE KOESTENBAUM

❦

"**A**n aria invented by a genius and composed with
taste is the masterpiece of music: here unfolds a
beautiful voice, here shines beautiful instrumental
music, here, as if unnoticeable, passion touches the
soul through the senses."
JEAN-JACQUES ROUSSEAU (1712-1778)

❧❧❧

"A Mozart quartet of voices is so complex,
so ingenious, so satisfying, so beautiful that we listen in
rising wonder inwardly applauding every cadence."
PAM BROWN, b.1928

❧❧❧

"Bach is higher mathematics,
a blessing to the mind and soul."
CHARLOTTE GRAY

❧❧❧

"Opera purges men of those hesitations and worries which make it difficult for them to acknowledge their importance to themselves. A good performance of an opera, that is, provides a language for us to speak of ourselves as we have always known we should speak."
HAMISH SWANSTON

"Opera convinces us that we are greater than we believed – capable of heights and depths that we had never known."
PAM BROWN, b.1928

ABOVE: ARBIT BLATAS, "SYMPHONY HALL"

PREVIOUS PAGE: PIERRE AUGUSTE RENOIR, "THE SMALL BOX"

"**O**pera is ephemeral. Even now, with superb recording techniques, nothing can hold the moment or convey the entente between audience and stage."
CHARLOTTE GRAY

❦

"But no amount of recordings... can quite prepare you for the live voice. Sitting in the dark shadows of an opera house way up in the gods, you are craning your neck struggling to make out which face and body is hers, when suddenly that tiny, round dot of a figure on the stage reaches out and strokes your ear."
JOANNA PITMAN, on Cecilia Bartoli

❦

"... it penetrated to every corner of the largest theatre or concert hall. People spoke of it creeping up to you and touching you. Audiences held their breath as they strained to catch the moment at which the note faded away into silence...."
JOAN BULMAN, on the pianissimo of Jenny Lind

ABOVE: ALISON CLARK, "BETWEEN US"

PREVIOUS PAGE: SPENCER GORE, "THE BALCONY AT THE ALHAMBRA, C.1912"

"One in fifty of those who attend our operas likes it already, perhaps, but I think a good many of the other forty-nine go in order to learn to like it, and the rest in order to be able to talk knowingly about it. The latter usually hum the airs while they are being sung, so that their neighbors may perceive that they have been to operas before. The funerals of these do not occur often enough."
MARK TWAIN (1835-1910)

೧⊙ல

"There is more nonsense talked in the crush bar of an opera house than anywhere else on earth...."
CHARLOTTE GRAY

Julian Alden Weir, "The Orchid"
Overleaf: Joseph Martin, "Art Nouveau–Winter Poster"

"**O**pera has the power to warn you that you have wasted your life. You haven't acted on your desires. You've suffered a stunted, vicarious existence. You've silenced your passions. The volume, height, depth, lushness, and excess of operatic utterance reveal, by contrast, how small your gestures have been until now, how impoverished your physicality; you have only used a fraction of your bodily endowment, and your throat is closed."
WAYNE KOESTENBAUM, from *Opera: A Penguin Anthology*

❧❦❧

"When people hear good music, it makes them homesick for something they never had, and never will have."
EDGAR WATSON HOWE

❧❦❧

" ... the older and steadier I get myself, the more I love opera. I like the plots complicated and the emotions enormous: heartbroken women pleading at the gates of monasteries; enraged gypsies swearing revenge; Venetian princes driven into exile; stout women expiring from consumption; stabbings; plunges off battlements; lovers being bricked-up alive by Egyptian priests; women dressed as men rescuing prisoners from dungeons – lead me to them! I wallow."
LIBBY PURVES

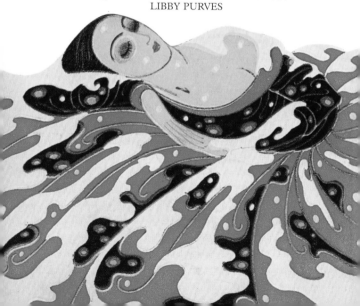

"The opera is the only refuge for poetry and fantasy. It is the unique place where the verse is still perceived, the last sanctuary of the gods, sylphides, nymphs, princes and tragic princesses; where uncouth reality is not admitted; it is a little world blazing in its gold and light... there is nothing of the actual, nothing of the real; one is in an enchanted world. The word is sung, the steps are pirouettes... an evening at the opera rests you from real life...."

THÉOPHILE GAUTIER (1811-1872), from *La Presse*, January 1, 1840

©1998 Max Oppenheimer, "The Famous Ros-Quartet"

"Music is a language by whose means messages are elaborated, that such messages can be understood by the many but sent out only by few, and that it alone among all the languages unites the contradictory character of being at once intelligible and untranslatable – these facts make the creator of music a being like the gods."
CLAUDE LEVI-STRAUSS, b.1908

We are the music-makers,
We are the dreamers of dreams,
Wandering by lone sea-breakers,
And sitting by desolate streams;
World-losers and world-forsakers,
On whom the pale moon gleams;
We are the movers and shakers
Of the world forever, it seems.
ARTHUR WILLIAM EDGAR O'SHAUGHNESSY (1844-1881)

Eva Gonzales, "An Italian Box at the Theatre"

"Opera... has great power to move the emotions. But the emotions have to be in the audience to begin with; the people must have something inside them that the performance will bring out."
LUCIANO PAVAROTTI, b.1935, from *Pavarotti: My World*

✧✧✧

"From the moment he stepped on to the stage the audience went wild. He flung his arms around Lucia, then left her only to return again in a frenzy of desperation. He had explosions of anger, then elegiac reflections of infinite tenderness, the sound, filled with sobs and kisses, escaping from his bare throat. Emma leaned forward to see him better, digging into the velvet of the box with her nails. ... She recognized all the ecstasies and anguish of which she had almost died. The singer's voice seemed like nothing else but the echo of her own consciousness, and this intoxicating illusion seemed at one with her own life. Surely no one on earth had ever loved her with such passion...."
GUSTAVE FLAUBERT (1821-1880), from *Madame Bovary*